Vashon-Maury Island Coloring Book

scenes drawn by Mair Alight

mair alight
transforming communication

Mair@MairAlight.com www.etsy.com/shop/empathyMair

I0150563

DUNLOP

Granny's Attic

an island tradition

VASHON INTUTIVE ARTS

1733

ISLAND CENTER FOREST

Jingle

Jingle

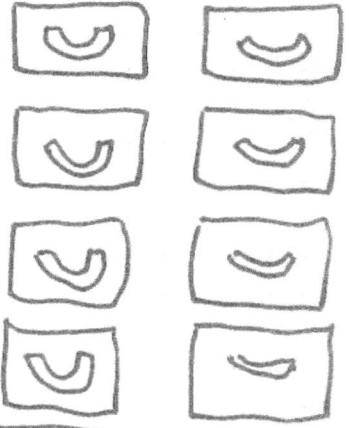

HERITAGE MUSEUM
Welcome!

Misty Isle Farms   Sheepdog Trial

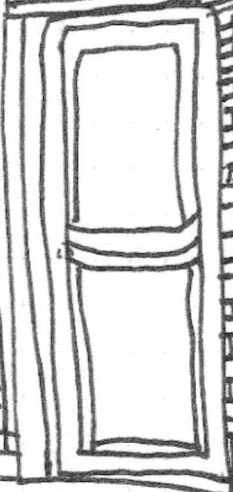

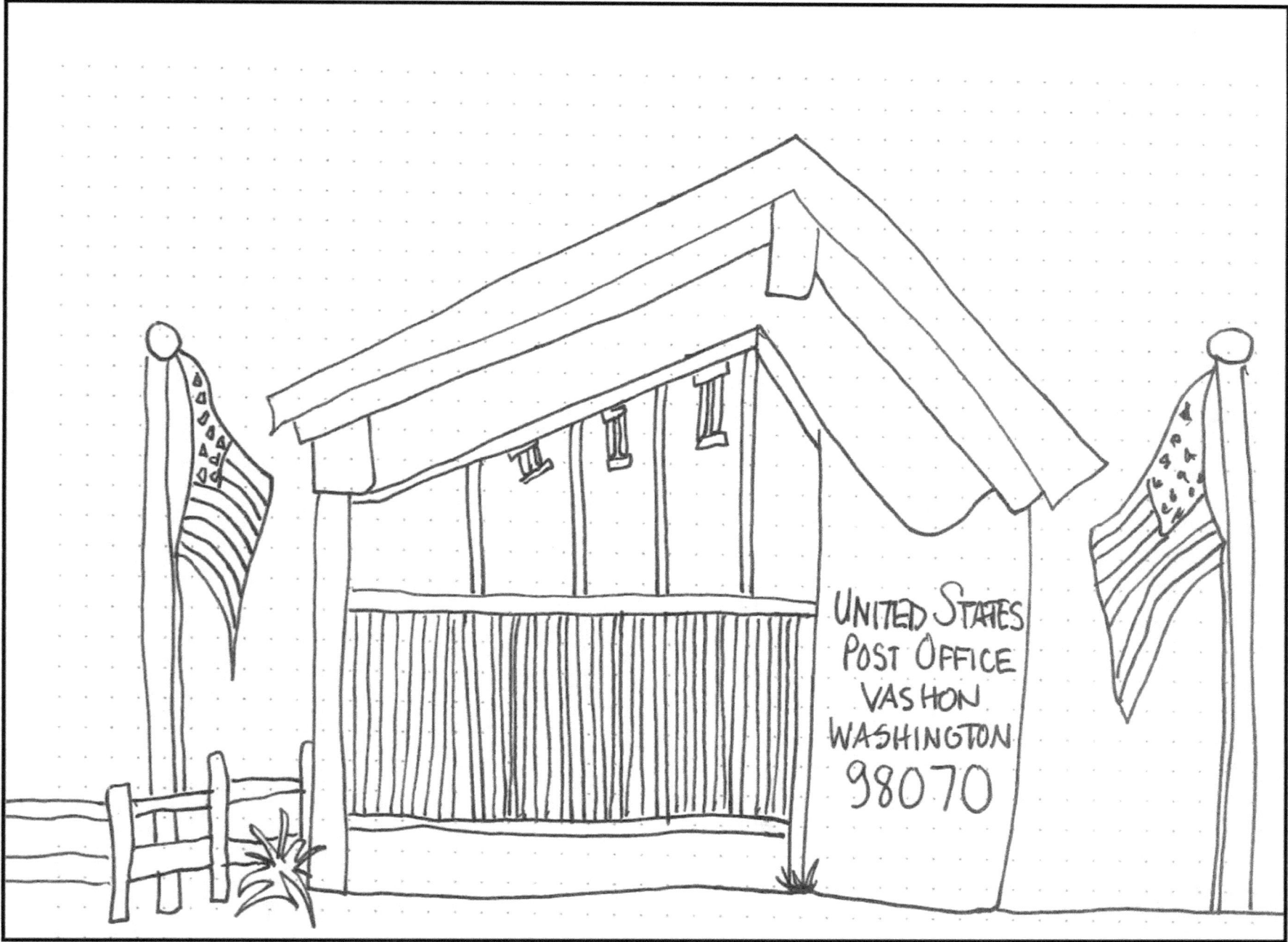

UNITED STATES
POST OFFICE
VASHON
WASHINGTON
98070

LOOKING OUT A VASHON WINDOW FROM HOME

VASHON YOUTH & FAMILY SERVICES

Identifying Information

1. **Burton Coffee Stand** 23908 Vashon Hwy SW
2. Burton Coffee Stand Flowers on the Wall
3. **Cafe Luna** 9924 SW Bank Rd
4. Camping
5. Garden Gate
6. Garden Hammock
7. **Granny's Attic** 17707 100th Ave SW
8. **Health and Wellness Fair-Table of Northwest Compassionate Communication - Vashon** www.NWCompass.org
9. **Island Center Forest** 363-acre working forest and nature preserve
10. Jingle 1
11. Jingle 2
12. **La Playa** - A Family Mexican Restaurant 10824 Vashon Hwy SW
13. Looking Out a Vashon Window From Home
14. **Lost & Found** and the Burton Post Office 23832 Vashon Hwy SW
15. **Minglement** 19529 Vashon Hwy SW
16. **Open Space for Arts and Community** 18870 103rd Ave SW
17. **Pt. Robinson Light** operational aid to navigation and historic lighthouse, located at Point Robinson,easternmost point of Maury Island
18. Sauna
19. **Snapdragon** 17817 Vashon Hwy SW
20. **South End Ferry** The Tahlequah terminal is located at the south end of Vashon Island
21. **Suds Laundromat** 17318 Vashon Hwy SW
22. **Thriftway** 9740 SW Bank Rd
23. **USPS Vashon Washington 98070** 10005 Southwest 178th Street
24. **Vashon Center for the Arts** 19704 Vashon Hwy SW
25. **Vashon Intuitive Arts** 17331 Vashon Hwy SW
26. **Vashon Library** 17210 Vashon Hwy SW
27. **Vashon-Maury Heritage Museum** 10105 SW Bank Rd
28. **Vashon-Maury Island Chamber of Commerce and Visitor Center** 17141 Vashon Hwy SW
29. **Vashon-Maury Senior Center** 10004 SW Bank Rd
30. **Vashon Sheepdog Classic** Misty Isle Farms
31. **Vashon Theater** 17723 Vashon Hwy SW
32. **Vashon Youth & Family Services** 20110 Vashon Hwy. SW
33. Waiting for the Ferry Oops! Gotta Go Vashon
34. **Zamorana** 17722 Vashon Hwy SW

www.ingramcontent.com/pod-product-compliance
Lightning Source LLC
LaVergne TN
LVHW081321060426
835509LV00015B/1620